THE MUSIC IN
THE FAIRY QUEEN

ENGLISH OPERA (1692)

The Drama adapted from
A Midsummer Night's Dream
by
SHAKESPEARE

The music by

HENRY PURCELL

EDITED BY ANTHONY LEWIS

VOCAL SCORE

NOVELLO PUBLISHING LIMITED

Order No: NOV 070320

PREFACE

Purcell's 'The Fairy Queen' was described as an opera when it was first produced in 1692, but in fact it belongs to that genre, characteristic of the 17th century English theatre, in which music and drama are combined, yet remain separate, instead of being fused together in an entity. Thus the dramatic part of 'The Fairy Queen' was a 17th century adaptation of Shakespeare's 'A Midsummer Night's Dream', but Purcell did not set a single line of Shakespeare. The text he set consisted of additions, mostly of the nature of short Masques at the end of each of the five acts. The relationship with the play was mainly through Titania and her attendant fairies, hence the title.

Ideally 'The Fairy Queen' should be performed on the stage, with both musical and dramatic components, but this is an elaborate and lengthy enterprise which, though it should be regularly undertaken, need not be the only method of presenting this 17th century masterpiece to a modern audience. For the music by itself is very well suited to concert performance, particularly if a narrator is used to set the scene from time to time. The context of each section of the music is given in the Purcell Society Edition of the full score.

The principal source of this edition is the contemporary Ms. full score, of which a large proportion is autograph, in the Royal Academy of Music in London. The following were also consulted:— British Council Library Ms. Op. 45, Gresham College Library Ms. VI. 5.6., *Some Select Songs in The Fairy Queen* (1692), *Ayres for the Theatre* (1697), British Museum Add. Ms. 30839, Royal College of Music Mss. 994 & 1144, *Comes Amoris* and *Orpheus Britannicus*. I would like to express my gratitude to all the authorities concerned for giving me access to this material.

In this vocal score all smaller-size music-type is editorial; this mainly relates to the continuo part, which has been written with the harpsichord in mind. Almost all the tempo-marks are editorial, and printed in italics; exceptions occur in nos 24 and 30. Except in nos 11 and 12, all dynamics are editorial. Suggested alterations of rhythm are shown in small notes above the stave.

Purcell indicates a large number of different roles in 'The Fairy Queen' but the work may be performed with a minimum of five soloists:— Soprano I, Soprano II, Alto or Countertenor or Tenor, Tenor, Bass. The orchestra consists of two recorders, two oboes, two trumpets, timpani, strings and continuo.

ANTHONY LEWIS

FULL SCORE AND ORCHESTRAL MATERIAL ARE AVAILABLE
ON HIRE.

CONTENTS

THE FAIRY QUEEN

FIRST MUSIC

PRELUDE

HENRY PURCELL

No. 1

19521

HORNPIPE

No. 2

SECOND MUSIC
AIR

No. 3

RONDEAU

No. 4

Allegretto

OVERTURE

No. 5

ACT I

DUET (*Soprano and Bass*) COME LET US LEAVE THE TOWN

No. 6   PRELUDE

Allegretto

(*reduction and continuo*)

mf (Vlns)

A

SOPRANO
mf

Come, come, come, come, let us leave, let us, let us leave the

BASS *mf*

Come, come, come, come, let us leave, let us leave the

mf
(Cont.)

p

Town, Come, come, come, come, come, come, come, come, let us leave,

p

Town, Come, come, come, come, come, come, come, come,

p

B

let us, let us, let us leave the Town. And in some___ lone - ly place, Where

let us leave, let us, let us leave the Town. And in some lone - ly place,

crowds_ and noise, where crowds_ and noise _____ were

Where crowds, where crowds_ and noise _____ were

ne-ver, ne-ver, ne-ver, ne-ver_ known, Re-solve _____

ne-ver, ne-ver, ne-ver, ne-ver_ known, Re-solve _____

_ to spend our_ days. Come, days. In plea-sant, plea-sant shades, _____

_ to spend our days. days. In plea-sant, plea-sant

SCENE OF THE DRUNKEN POET

SOLOS (*Soprano I and II and Bass*) and CHORUS

No. 7

PRELUDE

Allegro

DRUNKEN POET

f sempre liberamente, rubato e senza misura

Fi- fi- fi- fill up the bowl, then

(Cont.)

fi- fi- fi- fill up the bowl, then fi- fi- fi- fill up the bowl, then

1st FAIRY

mf

Trip it, trip it, trip it, trip it, trip it, trip it in a ring; a-

mf

round, a - round this mor-tal dance and

A

sing, dance and sing, dance and sing, dance and sing, a -

round, — a - round, — a - round _____ this mor-tal dance and sing.

CHORUS

SOPRANO
mp

Trip it, trip it, trip it, trip it, trip it, trip it in a ring; A -

ALTO
mp

Trip it, trip it, trip it, trip it, trip it, trip it in a ring; A -

TENOR
mp

Trip it, trip it, trip it, trip it, trip it, trip it in a ring; A - round, —

BASS
mp

Trip it, trip it, trip it, trip it, trip it, trip it in a ring; A - round, —

mp (Strs)

catch whom I may, catch, catch, catch, catch, catch, catch, catch, catch whom I may.

2nd FAIRY

A - bout him go, so, so, so, so, so, so, a - bout him go,

so, so, so, pinch, pinch the wretch from top_ to_ toe, from

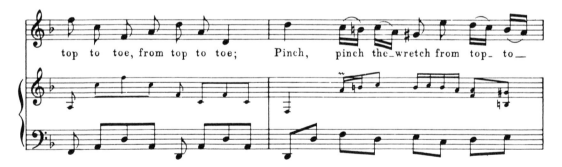

top to toe, from top to toe; Pinch, pinch the_wretch from top_ to_

D

toe; Pinch him for - ty,_ for - ty times, pinch him for - ty,_ for - ty

times, Pinch till he— con-fess his crimes, pinch, pinch,

pinch till— he— con-fess his crimes, Pinch, pinch till

he— con-fess his crimes.

CHORUS

A-bout him go, so, so, so, so, so, so, A-bout him go,

A-bout him go, so, so, so, so, so, so, so, A-bout him go,

A-bout him go, so, so, so, so, so, so, A-bout him go,

A-bout him go, so, so, so, so, so, so, A-bout him go,

so, so, so, Pinch, pinch the wretch from top _ to _ toe, from

so, so, so, Pinch, pinch the wretch from top to toe, from top to

so, so, so, Pinch, pinch the wretch from top _ to toe,

so, so, so, Pinch, pinch the wretch from top to toe, from top to

top to toe, from top to toe, Pinch, pinch the _ wretch from top _ to _

toe, from top to toe, Pinch, pinch the wretch from top to

from top to toe, from top to toe Pinch the wretch from top _ to

toe, from top to toe, from top to toe Pinch the wretch from top to

20

hold,   hold,   hold,   you   vile tor-ment-ing crew,   I

pinch till he_ con - fess his   crimes.

pinch till he con - fess his   crimes.

pinch till he   con - fess his crimes.

pinch till he   con - fess his   crimes.

(Cont.)

1st FAIRY

What, what,   what, what,   what, what,   what,

2nd FAIRY

What, what,   what, what,   what, what,what,what,what,

do, I do,   I do con-fess.

what?

what?

I'm drunk, drunk, as I live, boys, as I live, boys, as I

live, boys, drunk,_____ I'm drunk, drunk, as I live, boys, as I

live, boys, drunk, as I live, boys, as I live, boys,

[9]

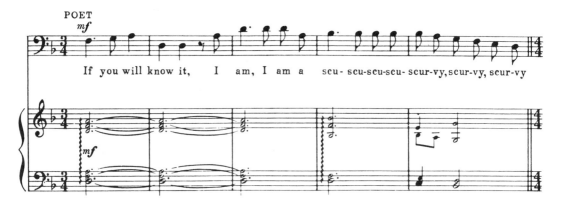

more, more, more, more, more,

con-fess, con - fess

more,

more, more, more, more, con-fess, con - fess,

con - fess, con - fess

more,

more, more,

more, more,

more, more.

more, more,

more, more,

more, more, more, more.

POET

I con-fess, I con-fess, I con-fess, I con - fess

I'm ve - ry, ve - ry,

ve - ry, ve - ry poor.

Nay pri - thee, nay pri - thee, nay

pri-thee now do not, do not pinch me so, Go- go- good dear—

de-vil let me, let me, dear— de-vil, let me— go; And

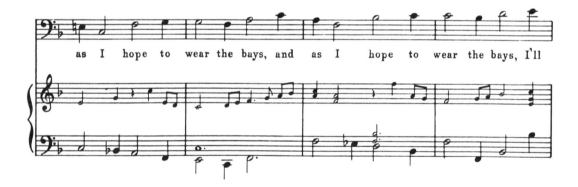

as I hope to wear the bays, and as I hope to wear the bays, I'll

write a son-net, I'll write, I'll write a son-net in thy praise.

FIRST ACT TUNE
JIG

No. 8

ACT II
SONG (*Tenor*) COME ALL YE SONGSTERS

No. 9
PRELUDE
Moderato

p (Strs)

mf

A

cresc.

poco f

Come all, come all, all, all, come all ye song - - - -

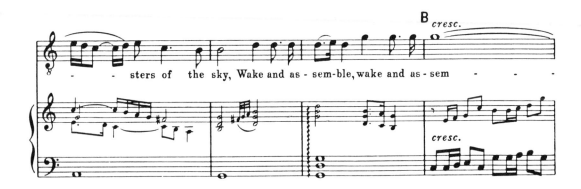

B

- - sters of the sky, Wake and as - sem - ble, wake and as - sem - - -

- - ble in this wood,

Come all, all, all, come all, all, all _____ ye song - sters

of ____ the sky, ___ Wake _____ and as-

sem - ble, wake _____ and as-sem - ble

in this wood: But

no ill-bo - ding bird ___ be nigh, No, none but the harm -

No. 10

Poco allegro

pp (Strs)

mf

E

F

p   cresc.   poco f

p   cresc.   f

segue

TRIO *(Tenor or Countertenor, Tenor and Bass)*

MAY THE GOD OF WIT INSPIRE

No. 11

ECHO

CHORUS NOW JOIN YOUR WARBLING VOICES

No. 13a

SONG AND CHORUS SING WHILE WE TRIP IT

No. 13b

Sing, sing while we trip it, trip, trip it, trip, trip it up-on the

green; Sing, sing while we trip it, trip, trip it, trip,

trip it up - on the green; _____ But no ___ ill va - pours

rise ___ or _ fall, But no _ ill va - pours rise ___ or _ fall, No,

no-thing, no, no-thing of - fend,__ no, no-thing of - fend__ our__ Fai - ry

Queen; __ No, no-thing, no, no-thing, no, no-thing, no, no-thing, of -

fend__ our Fai - ry Queen; __ No, no-thing, no, no-thing, no,

no-thing, no, no-thing of - fend __ our Fai - ry Queen.

Sing, sing while we trip it, trip, trip it, trip, trip it up-on the green;

Sing, sing while we trip it, trip, trip it, trip, trip it up-on the green;

Sing, sing while we trip it, trip, trip it, trip, trip it up-on the green;

Sing, sing while we trip it, trip, trip it, trip, trip it up-on the green;

green; But no ill va-pours rise or fall, But no ill va-pours

green; But no ill va-pours rise or fall, But no ill va-pours

green; But no ill va-pours rise or fall, But no ill va-pours

green; But no ill va-pours rise or fall, But no ill va-pours

no-thing, no, no-thing of - fend___ one Fai - ry Queen;___ No,

no-thing, no, no-thing of - fend___ one Fai - ry Queen;___ No,

no-thing, no, no-thing of - fend___ one Fai - ry Queen;___ No,

no-thing, no, no-thing of - fend___ one Fai - ry Queen;___ No,

no-thing, no, no-thing, no, no-thing, no, no-thing of - fend_ our Fai - ry Queen.

no-thing, no, no-thing, no, no-thing, no, no-thing of - fend_ our Fai - ry Queen.

no-thing, no, no-thing, no, no-thing, no, no-thing of - fend_ our Fai - ry Queen.

no-thing, no, no-thing, no, no-thing, no, no-thing of - fend_ our Fai - ry Queen.

FAIRIES' DANCE

ENTRANCE of NIGHT *(Soprano I)*, MYSTERY *(Soprano II)*,
SECRECY *(Countertenor or Tenor)*, and SLEEP *(Bass)*, with CHORUS of ATTENDANTS

No. 14

And all her peace - - ful train is near, That men to sleep in - cline. Let Noise and Care, Doubt and Des - pair, En - vy and Spite, (the fiend's de - light) Be ev - er, be ev - er ban-ish'd hence, Let soft Re -

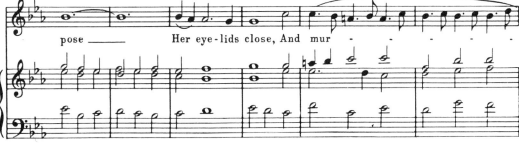

pose _____ Her eye-lids close, And mur - - - - -

-m'ring streams Bring pleas - ing dreams: Let

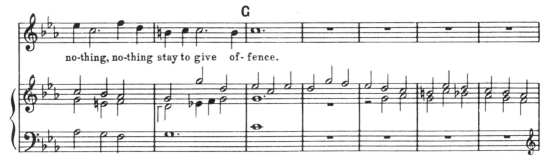

no-thing, let no-thing stay ___ to give of - fence, Let no-thing, let

no-thing, no-thing stay to give of - fence.

No. 16

SECRECY

One charm-ing night gives more_____ de-light Than a hun-dred, than a

hun-dred, a hun-dred, luck-y days. Night__ and__ I im-

prove____the taste, Make the plea - - - sure long - er

last,　　A thou-sand, thou-sand, thou-sand, thou-sand, thou-sand sev'-ral ways.

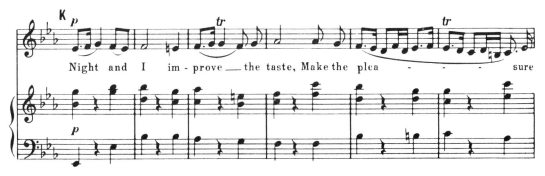

Night and I im-prove——the taste, Make the plea - - - sure

long - er last,　　A thou-sand, thou-sand, thou-sand, thou-sand, thou-sand sev'-ral

ways.

No. 17

Hush, no more, hush, no more, be si-lent, be si-lent, be si-lent all, Sweet Re-pose, sweet Re-pose has clos'd her eyes, Soft as fea-ther'd snow does fall! Soft-ly, soft-ly steal from hence, No noise, no noise dis-turb her sleep-ing sense, No noise, no noise dis-turb her sleep-ing sense.

CHORUS
pp SOPRANO
Hush, no more, hush, no more, be si-lent, be
pp ALTO
Hush, no more, hush, no more, be si-lent, be
pp TENOR
Hush, no more, hush, no more, be si-lent, be
pp BASS
Hush, no more, hush, no more, be si-lent, be
pp
si-lent, be si-lent all, Sweet Re-pose, sweet Re-pose has
si-lent, be si-lent all, Sweet Re-pose, sweet Re-pose has
si-lent, be si-lent all, Sweet Re-pose, sweet Re-pose has
si-lent, be si-lent all, Sweet Re-pose, sweet Re-pose has
p
N
clos'd her eyes, Soft_ as fea-ther'd snow does fall! Soft-ly, soft-ly,
clos'd her eyes, Soft_ as fea-ther'd snow does fall! Soft-ly, soft-ly,
clos'd her eyes, Soft_ as fea-ther'd snow_ does fall!
clos'd her eyes, Soft as fea-ther'd snow does fall!

DANCE FOR THE FOLLOWERS OF NIGHT

No. 18

Con moto
Canon four in two

SECOND ACT TUNE

AIR

ACT III

SONG (*Soprano*) and CHORUS IF LOVE'S A SWEET PASSION

No. 20

PRELUDE

Allegretto

SOPRANO

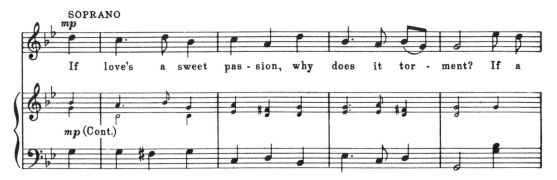

If   love's   a   sweet   pas - sion,   why   does   it   tor - ment?   If   a

bit - ter, oh — tell me whence comes my con - tent? Since I suf - fer with

plea - sure, why should I com - plain, Or grieve at my fate, when I —

know 'tis — in — vain? Yet so pleas-ing the — pain is, so — soft is the —

dart, That at once it — both wounds me — and tic - kles my heart.

SYMPHONY WHILE THE SWANS COME FORWARD

No. 21

DANCE FOR THE FAIRIES

Vivace leggiero

DANCE FOR THE GREEN MEN

SONG (*Soprano*) YE GENTLE SPIRITS OF THE AIR

No. 24

* The rhythm of the bass line has been altered to correspond with the suggestions for the voice part.

pre - pare, pre - pare

and join your ten - - - der voi - ces

here, ap-pear, ap-pear, ap-pear, ap-pear, pre-pare,

pre - pare, pre - pare

and join your ten - - der voi - ces here.

Soft, soft, soft _ as _ her _

sighs and sweet _____ as _ pear - ly

dew, and sweet _____ as _ pear - ly

dew.   Run, _____ run _

new di - vi - sions, run —— new di - vi - sions, and

such mea-sure keep, As when you lull, _ you lull _ the God of

Love a - sleep, ——————————— as when you

lull, _ you lull _ the God _ of Love —— a - sleep.

Da Capo

DIALOGUE BETWEEN CORIDON AND MOPSA

(Alto and Bass)

No. 25

PRELUDE

Allegro con brio

CORIDON

Now the maids and the

men are mak-ing of hay, We've left the dull fools, we've left the dull

fools, and are sto-len a - way. _____ Then Mop-sa no more be

* This dialogue also exists in versions for Soprano and Bass in F, with Mopsa's part transposed up an octave.

coy as be-fore, But let's mer-ri-ly, mer-ri-ly, mer-ri-ly, mer-ri-ly

play, __ And kiss, and kiss, and kiss, and kiss, and kiss the sweet time __ a-

MOPSA

_mf_

Why how now, Sir Clown, why how now what makes you so bold? __ I'd

way. __

have ye, I'd have ye to know I'm not made of that mould. __ I

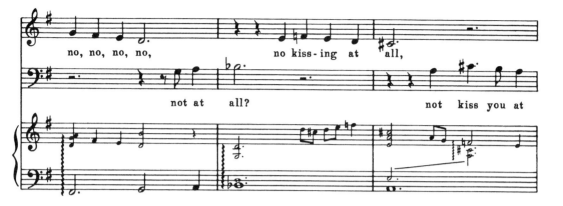

no, no, no, no,   no kiss-ing at   all,

not at   all?   not kiss you at

No, no, no, no,   no, no, no, no, no,   no; No kiss-ing at   all; No, no, no, no,

all?   why no?   why no?   why   no?

no;   I'll not kiss till I kiss you for good and all.

why no, no, no,   no, —————————————— no kiss-ing at   all?__ Slould you

give me a score, 'Twould not les-sen your store, Then bid me, bid me   cheer-ful-ly, cheer-ful-ly

kiss-ing at all, _____ I'll not kiss till I kiss you for good and all. _____

CORIDON

So small _ a re - quest you must not, you can-not, you shall not de - ny, _____ Nor

will I ad - mit of an - o - ther, an - o - ther re - ply. _____ You

MOPSA

Nay, must not, you shall not de - ny, you must not, you can-not, you shall not de - ny.

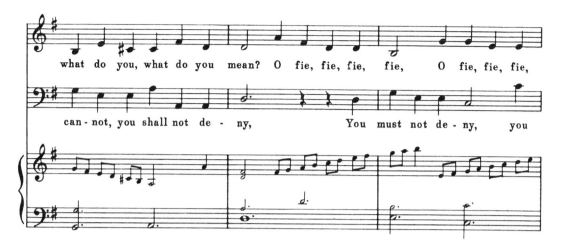

what do you, what do you mean? O fie, fie, fie, fie, O fie, fie, fie,

can-not, you shall not de - ny, You must not de - ny, you

fie, O fie, ___ fie, fie, fie, fie, fie, ___ fie,

must not, you shall not, you can - not, you shall not de -

fie, O fie, __ fie, fie, fie, fie, fie, __ fie, fie! Nay, fie.

ny, you must not, you can - not, you shall not de - ny. - ny.

No. 26 SONG (*Soprano*) WHEN I HAVE OFTEN HEARD

PRELUDE

Allegretto con moto

When I have of-ten heard young maids com - plain - ing That when men

pro-mise most they most de - ceive, Then I thought none of them

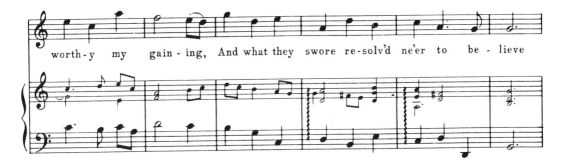

worth-y my gain - ing, And what they swore re-solv'd ne'er to be - lieve

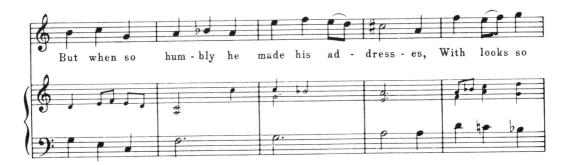

But when so hum-bly he made his ad - dress - es, With looks so

soft, and with lan-guage so kind, I thought it sin to re-

fuse his ca - res - ses; Na - ture o'er - came, and I soon changed my mind.

Should he em - ploy all his wit in de - ceiv - ing, Stretch his in -

ven - tion and art - ful - ly feign, I find such charms, such true

joy in be - liev - ing, I'll have the plea-sure, let him have the pain.

If he proves per-jur'd, I shall not be_ cheat - ed, He may de -

ceive him - self, but nev - er me; 'Tis what I look for, and

shan't be de - feat - ed, For I'll be as false and in - con-stant as he.

DANCE FOR THE HAYMAKERS

No. 27

SONG (*Countertenor or Tenor*) und CHORUS A THOUSAND, THOUSAND WAYS

No. 28

kind, so kind, so kind, so kind, no two shall

e'er be known so kind, No life so blest as ours, no

life so blest as ours, so blest as ours, so blest as ours, as ours, as ours, no life so

blest, so blest as ours, so blest as ours, so blest as ours, as

ours, as ours, no life so blest, so blest as ours, so blest as ours, so blest as ours.

* 'no life so blest' in Ms.

THIRD ACT TUNE
HORNPIPE

No. 29

Allegro con brio

ACT IV

SYMPHONY

No. 30

Allegro maestoso

f (Strs, Tpts, Timp.)

A

CANZONA

segue

cresc. - - - en - - -

- do   f

C

Fine

Adagio

mf (Strs)   poco f   p

pp

Dal Segno ℅ al Fine

SOLO (*Soprano*) and CHORUS NOW THE NIGHT

No. 31

all, all sa-lute the ris-ing sun, All, all, all, all, all sa-lute the ris-ing sun.

all, all sa-lute the ris-ing sun, All, all, all, all, all sa-lute the ris-ing sun.

all, all sa-lute the ris-ing sun, All, all, all, all, all sa-lute the ris-ing sun.

all, all sa-lute the ris-ing sun, All, all, all, all, all sa-lute the ris-ing sun.

mf

'Tis that hap-py, hap-py day, that hap - - - - - py

mf (Cont.)

day, The birth-day of King O-ber-on, 'Tis that hap-py, hap-py

day, 'tis that hap-py, hap-py day, The birth-day of_ King

* This semiquavere figure is more frequently shown in the R.A.M. Ms. with the last note D.

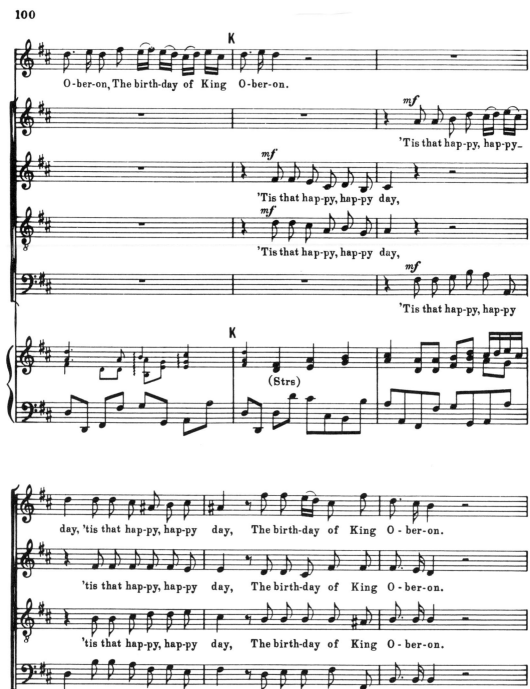

O - ber- on, the birth-day of_ King O - ber-on.

O - ber- on, the birth-day of_ King O - ber-on.

O - ber-on, the birth-day of King O - ber-on.

O - ber- on, the birth-day of King O - ber-on.

DUET (*Countertenors or Tenors*) LET THE FIFES AND THE CLARIONS

No. 32

ENTRY OF PHŒBUS

No. 33

SONG (*Tenor*) WHEN A CRUEL LONG WINTER
and CHORUS HAIL! GREAT PARENT

No. 34

PRELUDE

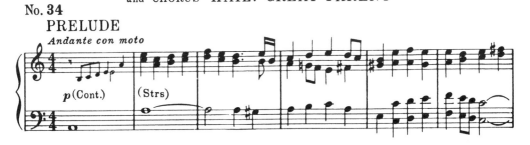

PHŒBUS

When a cru - el long_____ win-ter has fro - zen the earth, And

na-ture im-pris-on'd seeks in vain to be free, And na-ture___ im-pris-on'd seeks

Allegro

_____ in vain to be free; I dart forth my beams to give

all things a birth, Mak-ing Spring for the plants ev-'ry flow'r and each tree, I

tree. 'Tis I who give life, _____ warmth and

vi - gour to __ all, Ev'n Love who rules all things in Earth, Air __ and __

Sea, Would lan-guish and fade and to noth-ing, noth-ing would fall, The

world to __ its Cha - os would re - turn __ but __ for __ me. 'Tis me.

No. 35

Hail! Hail!_ great pa - rent, Hail! Hail!_____ great pa - rent

Hail! Hail!_ great pa - rent, Hail! Hail!_____ great pa - rent

Hail! Hail!_ great pa - rent, Hail! Hail!_____ great pa - rent

Hail! Hail!_ great pa - rent, Hail! Hail!_____ great pa - rent

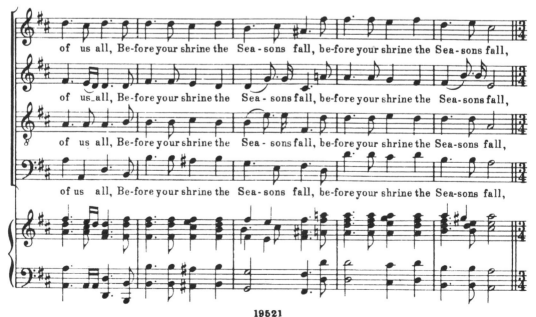

of us all, Be-fore your shrine the Sea-sons fall, be-fore your shrine the Sea-sons fall,

of us_all, Be-fore your shrine the Sea - sons fall, be-fore your shrine the Sea-sons fall,

of us all, Be-fore your shrine the Sea - sons fall, be-fore your shrine the Sea-sons fall,

of us all, Be-fore your shrine the Sea - sons fall, be-fore your shrine the Sea-sons fall,

SONG *(Soprano)* THUS THE EVER GRATEFUL SPRING

No. 36

Thus the ev-er grate-ful Spring,   thus the ev-er grate-ful

Spring Does her year-ly tri-bute bring, does her year-ly tri - - - - bute

bring, does her year-ly tri-bute bring, does her year-ly tri - - - bute

bring; All your sweets be-fore him lay, all your sweets be-fore him lay, Then round his

al-tar sing and play, All, all, all, all, all, all, all your sweets be-fore him lay, Then round his

al-tar sing and play, then round _____ his al-tar sing and

play. Thus the ev-er-grate-ful Spring Does her year-ly tri-bute

bring, does her year-ly tri - - - - bute bring, does her year-ly tri-bute

bring, does her year-ly tri - - - - - bute bring.

SONG (*Countertenor or Tenor*) HERE'S THE SUMMER, SPRIGHTLY, GAY

No. 37

Allegro moderato

SUMMER

Here's the Sum - mer, spright - ly, gay, smi - ling, wan - ton,

fresh ___ and_ fair; fair; A - dorn'd with all ___ the flow'rs of

May, Whose var - ious sweets per - fume_ the_ air; A - dorn'd_ with

all ___ the flow'rs of May, Whose var - ious sweets per - fume_ the air.

SONG (Tenor) SEE, SEE MY MANY COLOUR'D FIELDS

No. 38

ma - ny col-our'd fields, See, see my ma - ny col-our'd fields And load-ed

trees my will o - bey; All the fruit_ that Au - tumn yields,

All the fruit_ that Au - tumn yields I of - fer_ to_ the_ God of_ Day,____

_ All the fruit_ that Au tumn yields, ____ I of - fer_

to_ the God of Day. All the fruit_ that Day.

19521

SONG (*Bass*) NOW WINTER COMES SLOWLY

No. 39

numb'd with hard frosts and with snow cov-er'd o'er, Prays the Sun to re-

store him, prays the Sun to re-store him, and sings _____ as be - fore.

CHORUS

Hail! Hail!_ great pa - rent, Hail! Hail!_ great pa - rent

Hail! Hail!_ great pa - rent, Hail! Hail!_ great pa - rent

Hail! Hail!_ great pa - rent, Hail! Hail!_ great pa - rent

Hail! Hail!_ great pa - rent, Hail! Hail!_ great pa - rent

of us all, Be-fore your shrine the Sea-sons fall, be-fore your shrine the Sea-sons fall,

of us all, Be-fore your shrine the Sea-sons fall, be-fore your shrine the Sea-sons fall,

of us all, Be-fore your shrine the Sea-sons fall, be-fore your shrine the Sea-sons fall,

of us all, Be-fore your shrine the Sea-sons fall, be-fore your shrine the Sea-sons fall,

Allegro

Thou Thou who giv'st all, who giv'st all Na-ture birth, Thou who giv'st

Thou Thou who giv'st all, who giv'st all Na-ture birth, Thou who giv'st

Thou Thou who giv'st all, who giv'st all Na-ture birth, Thou who giv'st

Thou Thou who giv'st all, who giv'st all Na-ture birth, Thou who giv'st

Allegro

FOURTH ACT TUNE
AIR

ACT V
PRELUDE

No. 41

EPITHALAMIUM *(Soprano)* THRICE HAPPY LOVERS

No. 42

jea - lous-y;   From all that anx-ious care _____   and

strife _____   That at - tends _____   a mar-ried

life.   Thrice hap-py,   thrice hap-py,   thrice hap-py, hap-py, hap-py,

hap - - py, hap-py lov-ers,   may you be   for ev-er, ev-er,

ev-er, ev - - er free.

Be to one an - o - ther true, be to one an - o - ther true,

Kind to her, kind, kind to her as she to you; And since the

er - rors, since the er - rors of __ this night are past, May he __ be

ev-er, may he___ be ev-er, may he___ be_

ev-er, ev-er con - stant, she___ be ev-er,___

she___ be_ ev - er,___ ev - er,_ ev - er_ chaste,

may he___ be_ ev-er, ev - er con - stant,

she_ be_ ev-er,_ she_ be_ ev - er,_ ev - er, ev-er_ chaste.

SONG (*Soprano*) THE PLAINT

No. 43

ev-er, for ev - er weep!

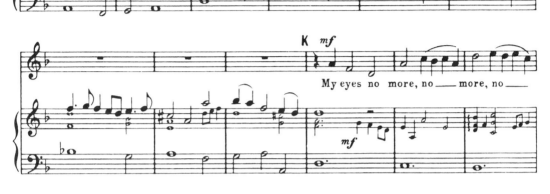

My eyes no more, no —— more, no ——

more, ——————— no more, —— no more —— shall wel - come sleep.

I'll hide me, I'll hide me from

the sight of day, And sigh, sigh, sigh my soul___ a -

way.

let me, O, O___ let me, let me weep!

O, O— let me, O, O— let me, let me weep! O,

O, — O— let me, for ev-er, ev - er weep, for ev - er,

for ev - er, for ev - er, for ev - er weep!

He's gone, he's gone, he's gone, his loss— de -

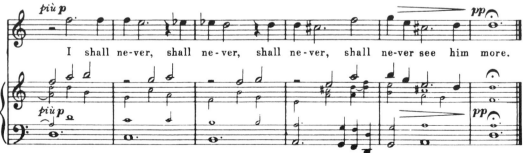

plore; he's gone, he's gone, he's gone, his loss__ de-plore, And I shall ne-ver, ne-ver,

ne-ver, nev-er, nev-er see him more,

I shall ne-ver, ne-ver, ne-ver see__ him more, shall ne-ver,

ne-ver, ne-ver see him more;

I shall ne-ver, shall ne-ver, shall ne-ver, shall ne-ver see him more.

ENTRY DANCE

No. 44

Allegro con brio

SYMPHONY

No. 45

SONG (*Tenor*) **THUS THE GLOOMY WORLD**

No. 46

A CHINESE MAN

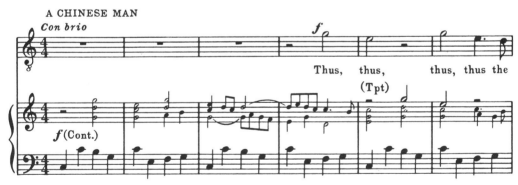

Thus, thus, thus, thus the gloom - - - y world at first ____ be - gan to shine,

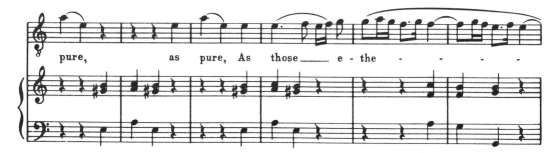

in in - no - cence— se - cure, Not sub - -

- ject to ex - tremes; There was—— no room then, no— room then for

emp - ty fame,— No cause— for— pride, no

cause— for— pride, am - bi - tion want - ed— aim,

am - bi - - - tion want'- ed aim.

SOLO (*Soprano*) and CHORUS **THUS HAPPY AND FREE**

No. 47

CHINESE WOMAN

Thus hap - py and free, thus treat - ed are we With

Na - ture's chief - est de - lights; ____ We nev - er cloy But re -

new our joy, And one bliss an - o - ther, and one bliss an - o - ther in - vites. __

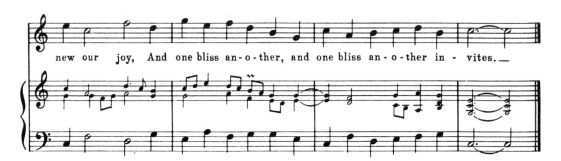

SONG *(Tenor or Countertenor)* YES, DAPHNE

No. 48

CHINESE MAN
Moderato

Yes,

Daph-ne, yes, Daph-ne in _____ your face I _ find Those

charms _____ by which my heart's be_ tray'd; Then let not your dis-

dain un - bind The pris'- ner, the _ pris'- ner that _____

_____your eyes have made Yes, made. She that in love makes

least de-fence Wounds _____ ev - er with the sur - est dart,

Beau-ty may cap - - ti-vate the sense, But kind - ness, but_

kind - ness on - ly gains the heart. She heart.

MONKEYS' DANCE

No. 49

SONG *(Soprano)* HARK HOW ALL THINGS

No. 50

Hark!   hark how all things with one sound

(Cont.)

re - joice,— re - joice,— re - joice,— re -

joice,_____

_____ re - joice,_ Hark! hark how joice,_ And the

world seems to_ have one voice, the world seems to_ have one

voice,_____

to ___ have one_ voice. Hark!

hark how all things with one sound _____ re -

joice,_ re - joice,_ re - joice,_____ re - joice_____

re - joice, re - joice, _____

re - joice.

SONG *(Soprano)* **HARK! THE ECHOING AIR**

No. 51

Allegro con spirito

(Tpt)

poco f

poco f

Hark!   hark! the ech-oing air a tri -

(Cont.)

umph sings, hark! the ech-oing air a tri - - -

- - umph sings, a tri - - - -

- - - - - - - umph, tri - umph

sings, _____ a tri - - umph, tri - umph

sings, Hark! hark! the ech-oing air a tri - -

umph sings,   hark! the ech-oing air a   tri - - -

- - umph sings,   a   tri - - - - - -

- - - - - - - umph, tri - umph

sings, _____   a   tri - - umph, tri - umph

sings,   And   all___   a - round,   and all___   a-

✳ Equal quavers sometimes in Ms.

round, pleas'd _____ Cu-pids clap their wings, clap, clap, clap, clap their wings, pleas'd

W **f**

_____ Cu-pids clap their wings, and all___ a - round, and all___ a-

round pleas'd _____ Cu-pids clap, clap, clap, clap, clap their wings, clap, clap,

clap, clap, clap, clap, clap their wings, pleas'd _____ Cu-pids clap, their

SOLOS (*Soprano I and II and Bass*) and CHORUS SURE THE DULL GOD

No.52

rouse __ him, we'll rouse __ him, rouse __ him rouse __ him with a charm.

we'll rouse __ him, we'll rouse __ him rouse __ him with a charm.

poco f

Maestoso   p   cresc.

Hy - men, ap - pear, ap-pear, ap-pear, ap-

p   cresc.

Hy - men, ap - pear, ap-pear, ap-pear, ap - pear!

Maestoso

p   cresc.

mf   cresc.

pear! ap - pear, ap-pear, ap-pear, ap - pear!

mf   cresc.

pear, ap-pear, ap-pear, ap - pear! ap - pear, ap-pear, ap-pear, ap-

mf   cresc.

f

Hy - men, Hy - men, ap - pear, ap-pear, ap-pear, ap - pear!

f

pear! Hy - men, ap - pear, ap-pear, ap-pear, ap - pear!

f

A
SOPRANO
ALTO
TENOR
BASS
p
cresc.
f
Hy - men, ap - pear, ap-pear, ap-pear, ap - pear! ap - pear, ap-pear, ap-pear, ap - pear!
Hy - men, ap - pear, ap-pear, ap-pear, ap - pear! Hy - men, ap - pear, ap-pear, ap-pear, ap - pear!
Hy - men, Hy - men, ap - pear, ap-pear, ap-pear, ap - pear! ap-pear, ap - pear!
Hy - men, Hy - men, ap - pear, ap-pear, ap-pear, ap - pear! ap - pear, ap-pear, ap-pear, ap - pear!
Hy - men, Hy - men, ap - pear, ap - pear, ap - pear, ap -
Hy - men, ap - pear, ap - pear, ap -
Hy - men, ap - pear, ap - pear, ap -
Hy - men, ap - pear, ap - pear, ap -

Segue subito

PRELUDE

No. 53

No. 54 SOLO *(Bass)* SEE, I OBEY
No. 55 DUET *(Soprano I and II)* TURN THINE EYES
No. 56 SOLO *(Bass)* MY TORCH INDEED
No. 57 TRIO *(Soprano I and II and Bass)* THEY SHALL BE AS HAPPY

hard-ly love out-lives ___ the wed-ding night, False flames, love's

me-teors, false flames, love's me-teors, yield my torch no light, no, no, no,

no, no, no, no, no, no, no, they yield my torch no light, False flames, love's

me-teors, false flames, love's me-teors, yield my torch no light, no, no, no,

no, no, no, no, no, no, no, no, no, no, no, they yield my torch no light.

pear   will on thy torch ap - pear,   ap - pear, will   on __ thy   torch ap-

on thy torch ap - pear, will on   thy   torch ap - pear, will   on __ thy   torch ap-

pear,   will on thy torch ap - pear.   pear.

pear,   will on thy torch ap - pear.   pear.

HYMEN *poco f*

My torch in-deed will from such bright -

Maestoso

poco f (Strs)

- - - ness   shine: Love ne'er had yet such al - tars, so di -

vine, _____ such al-tars, so di-vine, Love ne'er had yet, ne'er,

ne'er had yet such al - - - - tars so di - vine.

Allegro moderato

K 1st WOMAN

They shall be as hap-py, hap-py as they're fair; Love, love shall fill all, all,

2nd WOMAN

They shall be as hap-py, hap-py as they're fair; Love, love shall fill all, all,

HYMEN

They shall be as hap-py, hap-py as they're fair; Love, love shall fill all, all,

K *Allegro moderato*

f (Cont.)

all the pla-ces of care;— care; And ev-'ry time the sun shall dis-play His

all the pla-ces of care;— care; And ev-'ry time the sun shall dis-play

all the pla-ces of care;— care; And ev-'ry time the sun shall dis-play His

ris - - - ing light,— It shall be to them a new

His ris - - ing light,— It shall be to them a new

ris - ing, his ris - ing, ris-ing light,— It shall be to them a new

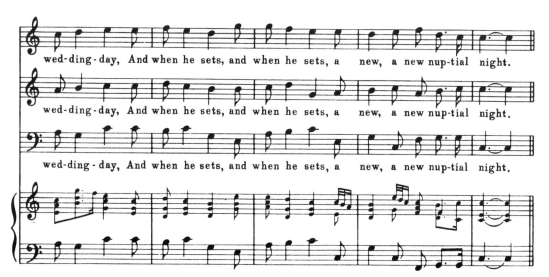

wed-ding-day, And when he sets, and when he sets, a new, a new nup-tial night.

wed-ding-day, And when he sets, and when he sets, a new, a new nup-tial night.

wed-ding-day, And when he sets, and when he sets, a new, a new nup-tial night.

CHACONNE

No. 58

CHORUS

No. 59

ris - - - - ing light,— It shall be to them a new

ris - - - ing, ris-ing light,— It shall be to them a new

ris - - - ing, ris-ing light,— It shall be to them a new

— His ris - ing, ris-ing light,— It shall be to them a new

wed-ding-day; And when he sets, and when he sets, a new, a new nup-tial night.

wed-ding-day; And when he sets, and when he sets, a new, a new nup-tial night.

wed-ding-day; And when he sets, and when he sets, a new, a new nup-tial night.

wed-ding-day; And when he sets, and when he sets, a new, a new nup-tial night.

Printed and bound in Great Britain by
Caligraving Limited Thetford Norfolk